Books by Lewis Burke Frumkes:

HOW TO RAISE YOUR I.Q. BY EATING GIFTED CHILDREN

MENSA THINK-SMART BOOK
co-authored by Dr. Abbie F. Salny

NAME CRAZY

What Your Name Really Means

LEWIS BURKE FRUMKES

A FIRESIDE BOOK • PUBLISHED BY SIMON & SCHUSTER, INC. • NEW YORK

MANUFACTURED IN THE UNITED STATES OF AMERICA
10 9 8 7 6 5 4 3 2 1

LIBRARY OF CONGRESS CATALOGING IN PUBLICATION DATA

FRUMKES, LEWIS BURKE.
  NAME CRAZY

  "A FIRESIDE BOOK."
  1. NAMES, PERSONAL—ANECDOTES, FACETIAE,
SATIRE, ETC.   I. TITLE.
PN6231.N24F78   1987   818'.5402   86-22042

ISBN: 0-671-63187-X

ILLUSTRATIONS COURTESY OF THE DOVER PICTORIAL ARCHIVE SERIES.

For
Mothy,
and Roysie,
Tim McGinnis
and
Dorothy Pittman,

all names
that have
special
meaning
for me.

NAME CRAZY

INTRODUCTION

Most people are sadly uninformed when it comes to the real meaning of their own and other names. Even when they take the time to research their names, they find the literature scant and that which there is uniformly wrong and muddled.

To wit, Isaac is attributed in one standard compendium to the Hebrew "exalted of the Lord," when in fact any onomast, as one who deals in names is called, knows that Isaac means "loving mallet" in Proto-Persian and was the common name given to second violinists during the fifth century.

No matter. In this book, in an attempt to set the record straight, I shall present, for the very first time, the true derivations of some of the more popular names now in fashion and thus amend part of the misinformation which so copiously abounds. I shall also play along with the movement away from gender identification by listing the names herein alphabetically rather than by girls' names and boys' names. If your name is "Irving," for example, you can look it up under "I," even though it isn't there because I left it out. But you get the idea. Alphabetical. It should also be apparent to almost everyone by now that names are made beautiful by what they mean, and by who wears them, rather than by which sex they adorn, though between you and me, Priscilla still looks better on Miss South Dakota than it does on Hulk Hogan.

So now that you understand what this book is all about, dive into it willy nilly (see page 123) and find out once and for all what your name *really* means. None of this "strong warrior," "gay flower" stuff! Here you get the truth, hard as it may be to swallow. Find out what your friend's name means too, and your sister's, and anyone else's name you've always wondered about. Frumkes happens to be my name, and enlightenment is my game. Enjoy.

LBF*

1986

---

* LBF holds a Black Belt in Onomastics from Harvard University and is licensed to practice names wheresoever the hell he chooses.

Aa

AARON   Aaron is Egyptian for "Sphinx-face," though many linguists dispute this and insist that Aaron means "camel vapor." Because of this unpleasant controversy, most Aarons are ashamed of their names and tell people they are Steven. If you meet a Steven who in every other respect looks like a "Sphinx-face" or a "camel vapor," chances are he is an Aaron.

ABE   Abe is short for Abernicus, the physicist brother of Copernicus, who developed the nuclear-pumped orgasm in 1236 and impregnated 200,000 women before he could be stopped. Most people, however, think that Abe is short for Abraham—which only proves once again how stupid most people are. Abernicus and Copernicus had two sisters, Suzernicus and Belindicus.

ACE Most psychoanalysts secretly yearn to be known as Ace (numero uno), but are afraid to have their names legally changed for fear that people will not take them seriously. "Appearing as discussants on tonight's panel are three distinguished members of our profession, Dr. Richard Frances, Dr. Meyer von Hemholtz, and Ace Goldin, who in addition to being the world's expert on imaginary children is a terrific shot in Marbles." So they continue to call themselves Fritz, or Meyer, or Sigmund, or Bela.

ADAM Biblical, "first man." The original Adam spent the better part of his life in pursuit of the knowledge of good and evil, which he eventually acquired. (It is good to love your brother. It is evil to put your brother's head in a vise and squeeze it until he apologizes for all the nasty things he has said to you, even though he probably deserves it.) Not to be confused with Atom, which derives from an altogether different source and is fissionable.

ADELE A little-known anagram for "Mississippi," Adele was the imp who bit Bronty the brontosaurus in the foot when he laughed, and then blew him away with the .45 magnum she had hidden in her purse.

ADINA Adina in Old Hebrew means "hot stuff," and there is no doubt that despite their quiet demeanor and bookish looks, Adinas are quite physical and frisky. The old Hebrews were not dopes, you know.

ADOLPH Unfortunately, Adolphs have been associated historically with butchers and meat tenderizers. This is unfair to the rest of the Adolphs, who are, by and large, gentle people. In German Adolph means "a-dolph" or "not-dolph," so we know right away that Adolphs are not dolphins. We also know, through logic, that they are not Cadillac Eldorados. What, then, are Adolphs? They are flower fairies, of course, and can be seen at twilight dipping their little tongues into the pollen and getting their noses all yellow. Next time you are in the garden round about dusk, see if you can spot any of the Adolphs. And if you do—squash one just for the heck of it and see what happens.

ADONIS Adonis, the Roman youth, looked like Sly Stallone and Arnold Schwarzenegger put together, only handsome like Cary Grant. So beautiful was he, in fact, that one day he exploded like a thousand suns, right in front of Medusa, whose snakes went crazy and turned him into a hat, with a wide brim, a size 7½. If your hat fits that description, you are most likely wearing Adonis.

ADRIAN Adrian is best remembered as a friend of Agoraphobic, the legendary Greek hero who was unable to leave his apartment during periods of stress.

AGATHA Agatha is the only six-letter name with three *A*'s in it, which is why the CIA uses it as the keystone for all its codes.

AGNES During the reign of Diocletian, Agnes was the young virgin who, in defiance of the soldiers of Rome, stood clothed only in her long hair and was raped 217,000 times. Thus Agnes has come to mean "50 cents each time, or 3 times for $1."

AL a.k.a. Big Al. Nobody is born with the name Al. You have to earn it the old-fashioned way, by carving your initials in your mother-in-law's forehead.

ALAN Alan is a middle name that sometimes pretends to be a first name. When you hear an Alan Kandell, for example, you know that it was originally Jeffrey Alan Kandell, or that Alan Footmaster, if truth be told, was really Robert Alan Footmaster. Alan is not a bad name, mind you, like Bart, or Stick, or Dumpstart; it just belongs in the middle.

ALANA "Beautiful skin" in Hawaiian. If you look carefully at an Alana, you will observe that her skin is like milk and rosewater. The one exception to this rule is Alana Kululana, of Maui, who is covered with unsightly blemishes from head to toe, the result of playing with toads as a child. Elanas, Illanas, and Olanas also have beautiful skin.

ALBERT The original Albert was Prince Albert in the Can, whom many of us remember fondly. Sad to say, Prince Albert was abused terribly by youngsters who called tobacconists at random on the phone and inquired whether the tobacconist had Prince Albert in the can. When the answer forthcoming was affirmative, they would respond, "Well, let him out," and hang up laughing sadistically. No one ever hears about Prince Albert in the can anymore, which is one of the great losses of our generation.

ALEXANDRA In French mythology Alexandra was so thin she could be used to jump-start a Buick left alone in a parking lot. When her husband left her to run off with Toulouse-Lautrec, Alexandra became depressed and sold herself on the streets as a magic trick.

ALICE Alice was the Greek goddess of public relations, who on a moment's notice could reverse anyone's destiny. Zeus, for example, was an umbrella salesman on Olympus prior to meeting Alice. Other clients included Odysseus, Jason, Achilles, and Cyclops, who without Alice would have been just another guy with one eye in the center of his forehead living alone in a cave. See Alice, 1 (212) 555-0946.

ALLEGRA A lesser character in Greek mythology, Allegra was either the Queen of Athens or a dinosaur. She is remembered best as the first woman to mix water with wine, or as an armored duckbill.

ALI The first term in "Ali Ali outs in free" is the Arabic version of "hide and go seek." Essentially the phrase means "Hear ye, hear ye, all of you still out there hiding. I'm not looking, so you can come out from under your camels and try and get to home base."

ALLISON Allison was one of the three weird tree gods in Norse mythology who hopped from branch to branch of the Great Pine Tree, Lundgwin, looking for kumquats.

ALMA Alma was originally Amla and has for centuries been a typographical error that has gone uncorrected. Oddly enough dyslexics get it right.

AMBER Amber means "love-cake" and has had that clearly defined meaning from time immemorial. Don't for a moment believe all that nonsense about its being fossil resin, clear reddish-yellow and containing bits of plants, feathers, flowers, insects, and so on, or that it was held to have magical and medicinal properties. It means love-cake pure and simple. End of story.

AMY Curiously, AMY is not really a name. It is the stock symbol for American Molybdenum Corp. of Yonkers which closed at 56½ yesterday, off ⅜ from Monday's high.

ANALYSAND In Greek mythology Analysand was the daughter of Neurosis, the Athenian mother who regularly worried where her children were at 10 P.M.

ANDY Andy was the Druid imp who could change himself into the shape of any letter. Thus when Gonthar threatened to bash him for removing his eardrums, Andy quickly changed into an H.

ANITA After the Iroquois maiden who could understand the language of the chipmunks and squirrels and articulate their needs to mankind. "More nuts."

ANN Ann was the sister of Na, the Egyptian river goddess who was swallowed by a garter snake when she was but a child. Profoundly affected by this experience, Ann mourned for her sister, but never let it get in the way of marrying for money. She divorced Nachem the wealthy Israeli developer and ran off with L'hotar the investment banker, who she imagined was even richer. With L'hotar she had three sons, Aknenaten, Thutmose IV, and Jerry Falwell.

APOLLO After the Greek god and civil rights activist who opened a variety theater on 125th Street in Harlem whence many a star began. In Spanish, a pollo is a chicken.

ARLENE Arlenes are soft, cuddly, and cute. Unfortunately, when left out in the sun too long they become incontinent. If you plan to be out in the sun for over twenty-four hours, dress your Arlene in a rubber suit.

ARNOLD Arnold was the first person ever to type faster than 600 words per minute. He did it on a souped-up IBM electronic 50 "Speedster" specially fitted to his fingertips. In 1967, during a charity type-o-thon, Arnold hit 800 words per minute on a racing Olivetti and flew into space. If you look up at the sky on any clear spring night, you will see Arnold typing in between Remonzo the Dog and the Portoclippiers.

ARTHUR Arthur was not only king of the Knights of the Round Table, but also the best poker player in the land. Legend has it that on any given day he could draw to an inside straight or pull a royal flush at will, sometimes even when he wasn't dealing. Thus, depending on which of his qualities one admires more, Arthur can mean either "slayer of dragons" or "big card cheat."

ATHENA The Greek goddess of war, wisdom, and sour cream, Athena was born in the usual way: when Metis became pregnant, Zeus swallowed her, and Athena sprang from his head, armed and fully grown. She maintained homes at Olympus, at the Acropolis of Athens, and at Boca West in Florida. In her later years, as her powers were ebbing, she became a patron to Belerophone, Perseus, Argus, and Bert Lance.

AUDREY Teutonic, "bride of the behemoth." No one is quite sure what this means, but it is thought that in olden days, an Audrey may have been married to a nose tackle for the Chicago Bears.

AVERY An avery is a place where birds are kept, a bird house.

AXEL In ancient Rome, Axel was the tragic centurion who got his nose caught in a grapefruit and died from an overdose of vitamin C. It was this story which inspired Edmund Wilson to write *Axel's Castle*.

Bb

BAAL One of those mood-lifting old aristocratic Phoenician names, like Blah and Blech.

BARBARA "Gorgeous underwear," in Persian. Look up a Barbara sometime. You'll be glad you did.

BEAU "The Deflowerer." Beau was the macho king of the Saxons who once attacked a bulletproof vest in his passion. When Winchell's daughter heard about this, she covered herself with butter and jumped into Beau's bed to hide.

BEN Ben was the infamous tooth fairy who was caught by federal authorities taking teeth from children even before they lost them. He was found out when little Willie McCormack noticed that all the teeth in his mouth were slowly disappearing and dollar bills were turning up under his pillow. Ben was sentenced to five years' hard labor cleaning a parakeet cage.

BENNO Ever since the president of Yale became "Benno," Benno has taken on a new respectability. In the old days Benno simply meant "He saw" in Latin, as in "Benni, Benno, Binki"—"He came, he saw, he conquered." However, today Benno has come to mean "blini stuffed with caviar and ricotta cheese," as in "Pass me one of those bennos, will you?" in French.

BERNIE Bernie was the god of pellagra and other intestinal disorders who in a fit of anger caused the sirens to come down with convulsive diarrhea. For years ships steered clear of the rocks no matter what the sirens sang, even rock favorites, until Odysseus, in compassion, sent a wineskin of kaopectate their way. Great Hera scolded Bernie for his antic ways, but Bernie laughed in her face. Even today, when your stomach goes on the blink, it may be that you in some way have offended Bernie.

BERT Biblical, "Lord knows." When confronted by a seemingly insoluble question, Old Testament characters would throw up their hands and go "Bert, bert!" Bert also means "happy flapjack" in Tuskaloosa prairie talk.

BETSY The name Betsy was coined in the late 1950s by a Belgian tennis pro who thought a particular Elizabeth looked good in tennis shorts and should have a name that reflected this quality. After much deliberation he chose "Betsy" over "Ummmmmmmmmm!" and the name took. Any Betsy who was born prior to the fifties is probably a Barbara and should stick to her bowling suit.

BEVERLY Beverly was the daughter of Smyrna, who blew marsh gas into the face of Zeus and was changed into a fig. Beverlys who are not figs are probably translucent.

BLAIR Blair doesn't really exist in any meaningful way. It's a peekaboo name, kind of ephemeral and diaphanous, and illusory. Now you see it, now you don't. That sort of thing. Like a quark, or will-o'-the-wisp, or calcium night-light eel. Most people come upon a Blair but once, and then aren't sure that they have.

BLAKE Flemish, "barking chocolate cake."

BLINCECAKE Blincecake was the brave warrior who rode a frog off into the night and was eaten by a carnivorous Buick on its way to Guam. Nowadays, however, Blincecake is just one of those names everyone else has, but you wish you had instead.

BLOOGPUSSY Federal law prohibits the dispensing of the meaning of this name without a permit. If you are still interested after being so informed, write to the author care of the publisher and he will try to accommodate you.

BOB Indian for "laughing bookplate," Bob is also the diminutive of Thumbob, Plumbob, Thingamabob, and Robert. Nobel Prize winners are seldom named Bob.

BON AMI Literally "good friend" in French. Bon Ami is the best friend a housewife ever had. The little chickens on it are cute and appealing. No one knows why Bon Ami has had such an effect upon society, it just has. Bon Ami is one of the great creations of all time, maybe even greater than the wheel.

BONNIE "Universal donor" in Fraternity-Speak. Bonnies are always among the first guests to be invited to toga parties. Sure of foot and delicate-smelling, Bonnies are classy lassies.

BOYCHICK Boychick was the brother of Apparatchik, which means "Shecky Greene" in Russian. During World War II, Boychick spearheaded the movement to grow longer wicks in candles.

BRAD Everyone who grew up in the fifties remembers Brad and Darb the palindrome twins, but few people remember that it was Brad who won the Johnny Mathis "sing-alike" at the sock hop and it was Darb who actually was Johnny Mathis. Brad also means "lip luster" in Transylvanian batterdrawl, while Darb means "luster lip." These are subtle distinctions, to be sure, but useful ones. See Darb.

BRENDA Old Irish for "lazy cow." Greeks and Gaels as well as ancients in many other lands saw great beauty in a young lazy heifer. Just why they saw such beauty is a question that has puzzled scholars for generations. The Brenda of Irish folklore was mother of the great Loofus, who "did slay the elfin hordes dressed only in Bermuda shorts." In her honor is named the River Brenda.

BRIAN Brian means "tough, rugged, quick, manly, athletic, and handsome" in Old Irish, and accurately describes men of that cut. While Brians make good linebackers, javelin throwers, and swimmers, they unfortunately are seldom long on brains. "And now, ladies and gentlemen of the American Physics Society, may I present Brian Merovikowicz, who will speak to you on 'Maxwell's Equations and the Lorentz-Poincaré Symmetry.' No, no, don't tackle me, dummy!"

BRUNO Bruno is a rare fragrance distilled from gymnasium lockers and stored in refrigerated lead containers. It is considered prestigious and precious in some circles, and men named Bruno frequently exude this quality openly and unashamedly. The Fabergé company recently purchased 12 grams of pure Bruno at a cost of $2.5 million.

BRYANT As in Gumble, or the park, Bryant in Middle English literally means "he who brys." During Chaucer's time many people "bryed," or baked clams in their shoe, and were considered curiosities at shore dinners. Today, with state-of-the-art ovens and cooking caldrons, Bryants are all but dying out.

BUNZEL Bunzel, with the accent on "zel," means "slow cheese" in every known language. An original, Bunzel must never be confused with Sludge or Fromage or, God forbid, Stuffing.

BURT Son of Nork, ruler of the planet Raydem in the Vegan Complex, once a common diem, now the Jephat of Jephats, wishes to meet attractive SWF, for possible romance.

Cc

CALEB Caleb Lipstroker was the polymathic turn-of-the-century industrialist who invented the all-weather bad-tasting thumb-condom to help children stop sucking their thumbs. It is also true that Caleb means "Park not" in New York traffic talk.

CALVIN Calvin was the peculiar Topfoot Indian who was larger than himself.

CAMPBELL See Doak.

CARL Carl, sometimes spelled Karl or Kkharl, was a demented Tofutti peddler in fourteenth-century Germany who was eaten by a Bavarian maiden without a name. His Tofutti lives on, however, a testament to his genius.

CARMEN In Bizet's opera, Carmen is the baseball player who tragically falls in love with third base. When the other players and the fans try to chase her off the field and away from her lover, Carmen picks up a bat and hits herself over the fence. In the final, heart-wrenching scene, Carmen is fined $50 for delaying the game.

CAROL Carol is an Xmas song, not a name. "Good King Wenceslas" is a carol, as are "Joy to the World" and "Silent Night." If you know someone named Carol, he/she is probably a song passing him/herself off as a person.

CAROLINE "Smart gumdrop" in Southern Drip Talk, Caroline was the golden-tressed princess in *Tales of a Butch Truckdriver-Killer*.

CASPAR A wimp name. Can you imagine anyone the least bit macho being named Caspar? You might as well be named Phyllis.

CATHY French. After Cathy of Aragon, the beautiful French wife of Ruppert Von Lohengrin, who due to an hormonal imbalance forgot she was married and slept with everybody in Germany. Quick to understand the biology involved, Ruppert buried his young wife up to her neck in red ants and then poured honey over her. See nymphomania, the crime and its punishment.

CATULLUS Popular name along Third Avenue. Catullus was the first-century-B.C. Roman lyric poet whose longest poem was an epic featuring the marriage of Peleus and Thetis; his shortest, the oft-repeated limerick beginning, "There was an old hermit named Sid . . ."

CECELIA Pronounced Chechelia, in Italian. Chechelia means "wax fruit" and encompasses the wonderful world of wax apples, pears, grapes, oranges, and bananas. If your name is Chechelia, and you spell it like that, with a "ch" running through it, chances are you are a wax fruit.

CECIL A small member of the weevil family (*Anthonus umbilicus*) which hides under long toenails until the time is propitious, then leaps out and eats your navel.

CECILY Shortened form of Cecilyopus, a hallucinogenic herb which the ancients put under their pillows at night to spice up their dreams.

CHARLES In French, a charle is a "freckle." Thus the oft-repeated phrase "She was covered with Charles" seems erotic at first, but on second glance describes a bespotted redhead.

CHIMERALDA After the mythological chimera which is described as having the head and breasts of a woman, the forepaws of a lion, the body of a goat, the hind legs of a griffin, and the tail of a dragon, and would be about the most hideous creature imaginable were it not for Irene Gonzola of East Islip, Long Island, who only last Thursday was mistaken for her own spleen. Irene's parents keep her locked in a can.

CHRIS One of those androgynous names that are so confusing. How do you know your Chris is a female? Maybe she's a "he" pretending to be a female. Maybe he's a "she" also playing a role. Maybe these two really believe they are the genders they are portraying. How can you be sure? Answer: you can't. Even if you squeeze them you can't be certain. So play it safe; date a Judy, a Linda, or a Marsha. These girls may not be as exciting, but at least they know who they are.

CLAIR Clair is always short for "Clairvoyant." If pressed, most Clairs can not only tell you your past and present, they can tell you your future, which numbers you need to win the lottery, and who the dark gentleman is that's about to change your life. Ask too about the new rates on the Orient Express.

CLARK After Clark Kent, the *Daily Planet* reporter who, paralyzed by excitement, stood by idly while Superman tickled and whipped Lois Lane.

CLAUSTROPHOBIC The stalwart Greek hero who would hyperventilate in chariots and huts, Claustrophobic has come to mean "brave chair" and is usually adopted by people who exhibit this quality.

CLIFF Cliff was the brother-in-law of Stan, so called because he bestowed upon humankind the three basic food groups, hamburgers, pizza, and M&Ms.

COKEHEAD Cokehead was to the Dalton Gang essentially what Thumper was to Bambi and friends.

COLE Cole is old Gaelic for "Tree frog or eggplant? Choose!" No one really understands what this means but nine out of ten people choose eggplant.

CONAN According to the Celtic myth, Conan was the steel-muscled warrior who in moments of unusual sensitivity would crush billiard balls to hear them squeak. Highly intelligent, he finally solved the riddle of the sphinx with his fist. See Dork.

CONRAD "Bold egg salad" in Vietnamese.

CONSTANCE One of the major astrological signs. People born under Constance, the Steel-Belted Parsnip, are prone to bouts of prognesia and remalgia in the spring. The antidote seems to be spelling backward at speeds above 600 words per minute.

CORDELIA In German mythology, Cordelia was the sad Rhine maiden who tried to swallow herself with a glass of water, but ended up choking on her nose. In time her psychiatrist reduced her sessions to 200 times a week.

CORNELIA A bluish flower in the Aster family that plays "I'm a Yankee Doodle Dandy" when its petals are pulled off.

CORONARY Coronary is a stupid name for anyone to give to a child, since it is usually associated with heart attacks. Nevertheless, some parents insist on naming their children Coronary on the off chance that it has something to do with kings and queens and being crowned.

CRAIG Latin, "gay woodchuck."

CYNTHIA According to fifth-century theoretical Christianity, Cynthia played second harp in the celestial orchestra. She would also cross her eyes every time she snorted cocaine.

CYRIL Gaelic for "lycanthrope." All people named Cyril have a congenital predisposition to turn into a werewolf when you're not looking. Never turn your back on a Cyril, unless, of course, it has already eaten.

Dd

DAISY "BB gun," in American adolescent. Daisy was also the daughter of Menemsha, who had no Social Security number.

DALE The senior partner of Hill & Dale, who represented Oedipus in the paternity suit brought by his mother. Female Dales are almost irresistible.

DANA Assyrian-Babylonian for "prune Danish," the dana was much loved among constipated Assyrian-Babylonians, who ate danas constantly and carried them in their purses and wallets. The line "The Assyrians came down like the wolf on the fold" is not an inaccurate description of Assyrian soldiers, who after a few danas became crazy like wolves—arrghh!

DANIEL Daniel, or Dan, is the force that holds peanut butter together and prevents it from exploding in all directions at once, like a supernova, and destroying the universe.

DANIELLE The beautiful French seer who correctly predicted that Benjamin Franklin would rise up from the grave to eat Menudo.

DARB See Brad.

DARWIN Is almost always a misspelling of "Darwig," a plant grown by Indians for medicinal purposes. The Silver Lace Darwig was used by the Indians to prevent Athlete's Nose, a condition similar to La Tourette's Syndrome, wherein the afflicted brave would fungo balls out to the field with his nose, or punch other braves with his nose, not even realizing that he was doing so.

DAVID David was the Old Testament hero who as a youngster slew the Philistine bully Goliath of Gath, not with a slingshot, as most people think, but by tying the giant's testicles to his bicycle chain and riding forty miles into the desert. Feeling chastened for his erring ways, Goliath converted to Judaism and was immediately given two dress businesses and some real estate to start him on his way.

DAWN After the morning phenomenon whereby garbage trucks and cars honk their horns loudly until people go crazy and get out of bed and get rifles and start firing at the goddamn things.

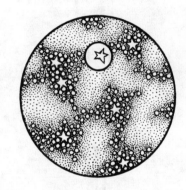

DEBBIE Sanskrit for "warm lymph node." Debbie is also the northmost star in the constellation Cream Cheese, 200 million light-years from our own Milky Way. In Old Welsh, Debbie was the sister of Gryfnis, the foolish farmer who sprayed Windex into the eyes of a wolf.

DELMORE Delmore was the first person ever to have seriously believed he was a fried egg. For more than thirty years he took this delusion from analyst to analyst trying to rid himself of his ridiculous affliction, but to no avail. At the age of 50 he was apprehended by a police officer who caught him molesting an English muffin, and was sentenced to five years' hard labor at a federal penitentiary. He finally died of a broken yolk. If your name is Delmore, you should consider changing it. Salmore is a nice name.

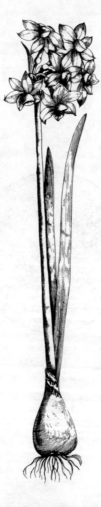

DENISE Denise was the sister of Narcissus who was so beautiful that she fell in love with herself and eloped. On her honeymoon she had great difficulty consummating the marriage, and spent two frustrating weeks chasing herself around the room. Eventually she wasted away and became a flower.

DENNIS Spell it backward and find out what Dennis did.

DESIRÉE Desirée was the last woman to smoke an unfiltered cigarette. The cigarette was an old-fashioned Lucky Strike, and she smoked it on April 27, 1983.

DIANE Old French-Indian name meaning "cute fruitcake." Dianes invariably kiss on the third date. The one exception to this rule was Diane of Aquitaine, who was congenitally number-blind and thought every date was her third date. Occasionally a Diane will pronounce her name "Dee-*on*" to let you know she has higher standards. Trust me—third date.

DOAK See Campbell.

DOMINIQUE Mistress of night, singer of songs, from Hydra, seventh moon in the Red Giant Calcium Cluster, wishes to meet SM jephat of jephats, 35–45, into whips, nets, electric probes, and chains, for good old-fashioned fun. No kooks.

DONALD It's hard to escape the connection with Duck, but there have been Donalds who were laser scientists, and brokers, and architects. However, if you have three nephews named Huey, Dewey, and Louie, whatever I say isn't going to mean much.

DONNA After the eighth-century martyr who was refused a charge card at Bonwit Teller. Donna has come to mean "she who pays cash, but not by choice." Perhaps in compensation, Donnas invariably have good legs.

DOROTHY Name created by Aunt Em in *The Wizard of Oz* for her niece who really had no name and was called "Niece" by everyone who knew her. Dorothy has come to mean "she who makes it with scarecrows, tin men, and lions." Other variations; Dorothea, Dorthea, Dortha, and Niece.

DOUGLAS Douglas was the Viking god of creamed soup. Crossing the fjords on a cold, blistery day in December, many a Viking prayed to Douglas and was rewarded every now and then with a cream-of-mushroom soup or sometimes cream-of-tomato. If Douglas didn't answer their prayers, the Vikings would throw the runes to get his attention, and complain loudly. If the runes were graphic enough, Douglas would throw a cold vichyssoise at them.

DUANE Duane derives from the name of the powder, invented in the ninth century, that prevents Japanese Sumo wrestlers from smelling like cow pastures. Yuki Nagasaki, a 400-pound Sumo, forgot his duane in the spring of 1944 and cleared the entire territory east of Osaka. Duane is a very important name in Japan.

DUDLEY A dudley is a small sheep specially bred in Central China to fight battleships. Because of these sheep, which have armor-piercing teeth and hate battleships like the devil, Central China has never lost a major naval encounter. Left unharnessed though, dudleys are dangerous, and have been known to chew up a PT boat or destroyer just for the fun of it. Recently the Chinese have been outfitting some of their better-swimming dudleys with snorkles to hunt subs.

DYLAN Dylan was the legendary Irish track star who could run faster than a cheetah. That, of course, is what Dylan said, and Dylan was a pathological liar. Make of it what you will.

Ee

EARL "Oil" in Old Brooklynese. People who genuinely know Old Brooklynese also pronounce terlet "toilet."

EDITH Edith was the Norse goddess of light. When Edith went to bed, everything was dark. When Edith got up, everything was light. People would say, "Get Edith up, will you? I can't see a thing." Soon manufacturers caught on and began to make little ediths that people could carry with them on camping trips, and into the garage. They would store their ediths in the closet until they needed them; then in a blackout, or other emergency, they would wake up the edith. In time they even made disposable ediths and rechargeable ediths. Next to Brünnhilde, the goddess of pizza with sausage, Edith was the most popular of all the Norse goddesses.

EDWARD After Edward VII, who was the first king of England ever to assemble a major cauliflower collection.

45

ELAINE In *The Tempest*, Elaine was the Nymph Queen who kissed Oberon when he wasn't looking and changed him into a Rand McNally road atlas.

ELEANOR The real name of the great leader of the FBI who posed for his entire life as J. Edgar Hoover.

ELI Hebrew, "long kneecap." Elis are the mirror images of Iles who are rare Jewish trayf-eating elves.

ELIZABETH Elizabeth of Nesselrode was the English princess who, for lack of anything better to do, poisoned her country's water supply in 1764. It is because of this deranged act that England today has no population.
Note: The Corinthians, who now occupy England, all drink tea.

ELLEN Latin, "she who puts lamprey eels in other people's beds."

EMILY The martyr who allowed herself to be publicly stuffed and roasted on November 25, to dramatize the plight of Thanksgiving turkeys.

ENOCH A cross between Enid and Warlock meaning "He knocks," Enoch is a popular name among the English drinking class.

ERIC Eric, or "durkmaster" in Dutch, is considered an aristocratic name among Eastern Seaboard yuppies. The reason for this is that most E.S. yuppies want their children to grow up to be durkmasters.

ERICTHONIUS or Erectheus II. Sometimes preferred over Eric for its musicality. Ericthonius consulted an oracle in order to defeat the Eleusinians. The oracle told him to sacrifice his daughters and to play Polyphemus Hanover in the fifth. The results of these endeavors are known as the Eleusinian Mysteries. In recent years, archaeologists and historians have uncovered evidence which suggests that Polyphemus Hanover ran out of the money.

ERNIE Ninety-eight percent of all Ernies are fullbacks, boxers, or wrestlers. The other 2 percent work the margarine pits of South Carolina.

E.T. E.T. has become the name of choice among Steven Spielberg fans. Another version of this name that is rapidly catching on is E.S.T., which means Extra Special Terrestrial. These people look like the other E.T.s except they can fly.

EUGENE Eugene, pronounced yuJeen, is a new kind of lighter fluid which is reputedly superior to wood logs. Eugene has also been used as racing fuel in toy bunny rabbits, though this has been shown to burn out their kishkas. If your name is Eugene you run the risk of being labeled U-E, which is thought undignified for doctors and political candidates. "Hey, Doctor U-E" . . . it becomes complicated.

EVAN Evan, or "Chum Chum Chop" in Mandarin, is a name associated with high-I.Q. Chinese field peasants who work the paddy fields in their native land but almost always send their kids to Loomis, Choate, or Exeter.

FAITH The Latin acronymn for "Fidelity And Intuition Take Hold." Thus people who profess to know where they are going in the dark have "faith." St. Polypf of Uffizi, who couldn't pronounce his own name, had faith, and walked into a well.

FAY Fay was the Persian goddess of carburetors who lay dormant for centuries until the invention of the automobile by Burt Reynolds in 1438.

FLORENCE Florence was the slow Italian virgin who thought that eating green olives before bedtime would prevent pregnancy. After twelve children and three abortions, she realized, too late, that it had been black olives all along.

4² 42, as you probably know, is a number. But if you happen to have a number instead of a name, 42 is a hell of a number to have. Congratulations.

FRANCES Frances is the feminine for "Francis," which is the masculine for "Frances," which is the feminine for "Francis," which is the masculine for "Frances," which is the feminine for "Francis." The German mathematician Von Sorce once carried Frances out to 312 places.

FRANK Preferred for some reason over the original Teutonic "Frunk," Frank has become the name of choice among truck drivers, moving men, and world-class garage mechanics. In most cases if you look at a Frank closely you will notice that he has big forearms and a tattoo. If he has neither, he is probably a Terry or a Jimmy.

FROGUAP In a nationwide survey conducted in 1986, Froguap was found to be the ugliest name in the English language. Chuck came in second.

Gg

GABRIEL Of all the archangels in the heavenly pantheon, Gabriel was the only one who was fluent in both French and Pig Latin. Because of this, God made Gabriel a life member of the Bath and Tennis Club.

GAIL After the great Westchester shopper who, in 1986 alone, established new world records in sportswear, evening clothes, bone china, and lawn furniture.

GARY Gary was the spitball imp in Radium Jewett's *The Lunar Classroom*. Garys are generally good-looking, with tousled dark hair and long eyelashes and much sought after by girls. The one exception to this rule is Gary Barky of Cambridge, Mass., an ugly sonofabitch who sexually attacked a baseball bat while on loan from one psychiatrist to another during the 1983 patient-trading season.

GEORGE All Georges are descended from Saint George, the fourth-century hero who defeated a dragon in hand-to-claw combat. George caught the dragon by the tail and whipped him against a tree. On the rebound he whacked him in the gullet with a forearm smash, then picked him up and body-slammed him into a ravine. When the dragon tried to get up, George kicked his fire out. George was some kind of guy.

GEORGIA Latin, "Alabama."

GERTRUDE Gertrude was the eldest of the five Gillicle sisters, Gertrude, Millicent, Lillian, Priscilla, and Lydia, who couldn't say their names fast ten times. Gertrude Gillicle, Gertrude Gillicle, Gertrude Gillicle, Gertrude Gillichle, Gerturude Gillicchle, Gertood Gilltitlicle, Gerchoof Gilliccelloel, ghhhhllllilcilekjjjjj!

GIL Gil was the Roman god of black ink. His twin brother, Hiram (Tsuriss in Yiddish), was the god of red ink, and was responsible for hundreds of Roman companies' going belly up in bankruptcy. Company accountants and presidents today still fear Hiram like the plague and pray to Gil.

GLENN In Swedish mythology Glenn was the little clothespin imp you could wear on your nose to ward off radishes. Many parents of Swedish descent still name their children Glenn if they have an abiding fear of radishes, and wear them on their noses.

GLORIA Latin, "Bright noose." Gloria was also the lesbian warlord in *Amazon Mission to Earth,* by Lady Rapunzel Dwicker.

GOOMDRAGON Goomdragon is one of those old traditional names that parents from Boston, Main Line Philadelphia, and New York give to their kids before sending them off to prep school, and then Yale or Princeton. There have been more Goomdragons in Skull & Bones than I can count: ditto with Hasty Pudding. If you're into blue blood and lineage, consider Goomdragon seriously for your name.

GRETCHEN German, "Scratch my back." In Germany, in spring, it is commonplace to hear lovers going "Gretchen, Gretchen." Verstehen Sie? Gretchens are people of action and romance. Never confuse Gretchen with Gritchen, which is a foot fungus. And never Gretchen anyone's Gritchen.

GRID "Grape," Swedish. See Ingrid.

GUNGA DIN Gunga Din was the son of Sarah and Morris Din from the Five Towns. He was a shy, unassuming boy, a poor student, and an annoying one who somehow found his way into Kipling's poem. Other than that, he never amounted to anything, as was expected, and Sarah and Morris continued to be ashamed of him. He had two brothers, Bunga and Wunga, who were even less successful than he was, and they smelled bad.

Hh

HAROLD Adnan Khashoggi's yacht.

HARRIET Harriet was the American Psychoanalytic Society's unanimous choice as "Patient of the Decade" in 1979. So improved was Harriet that her analyst decided, there and then, to stop dipping her in Russian dressing.

HARVEY Liverpool English for Arvey, a rich mix of okra, cranberries, and lug nuts, which is being test-marketed by Arvey Inc as a "real man's" dip. Arvey Inc also produces "Larvae," which is considered extra macho and makes even strong men go "Yuck!"

HATCHRAVEN See Wingstabler.

HEATHER Heather was the controversial Hawaiian medical researcher who exploded the theory that grass skirts could lower blood cholesterol. Heather was killed in a freak accident in 1979 when a coconut she was carrying in her purse jumped out and swallowed her.

HECTOR According to legend, Hector was the last person to sleep with Helen of Troy.

HELEN "Jelen" in Spanish.

HENRY After Henry of Aragon, the only person who got *The New York Times* in color.

HERB Herb was the name of the Rebel soldier who was forced to become an Oklahoma "Sooner" after he shot his teeth into a neighbor's house. Depressed and humiliated over no longer being a Rebel, Herb spent his remaining days trying to find out what a Sooner was.

HILARY A name invented by the Roman poet Ovid to rhyme with Gilary.

HIRAM Yiddish, "Tsuriss."

HOLLY According to the *Nibelungenlied*, Holly kissed Polident on the lips and was forced, as punishment, to dribble a basketball from New York to Seattle.

HOPE In the *Satyricon*, Hope was the angel who had her name legally changed from Dope.

HOWARD Howard was the name of The Force in *Star Wars*.

HUGH "How" in English English. "Hugh do you do?" or "Hugh are you!" or better yet, *Hugh to Raise Your I.Q. by Eating Gifted Children*. That last is a great book by yours truly; go out and buy it.

Ii

IAN Ian was one of the four giants in *Richard the Third*: Megabuck, Gongoltha, Hulkster, and Ian. Or was it in *Daniel Deronda*?

INGRID Swedish, "seedless grape." See Grid.

IRENE While it is true that many Irenes are irenic, or peaceful, types, the name Irene actually means "strong like iron, ugh! tough," which makes one wonder why more men aren't Irenes. Maybe they are.

IRIS Iris was the beautiful daughter of Joan Collins and Crazy Eddy who purely by accident poked Zeus in the eye with a hanger. Avuncular and forgiving by nature, Zeus responded by turning Iris into a container of decaffeinated coffee. Later, having reflected some, Zeus changed her into a melon. For all we know he may change her tomorrow into a raincoat lining.

IVOR   A corruption of the Russian Igor, which means absolutely nothing. Ivor of Roumania was the great sportsman who hunted elk with his breath.

Jj

JACK The original Jack from the "beanstalk" story is chased across the Doomenland by a crazy bald head who thinks he is a hat. When Jack finally escapes into an open electrical socket, Mr. Zism pulls the switch and gives him 300,000 big ones right across the beam, turning him into an ash. This is the first appearance anywhere of a Jack ash.

JACKIE Jackie is Flemish for "plaything." If you know Flemish, "Kreuzen oigle Jackie!" Ha, ha, ha!

JAMES James is a chauffeurian name, out of the same bottle as Huffsnail and Barkwell. Even if James is a Wall Street baron or an English king, people will say, "Home, James."

JANE One of the four caustics; potash, soda, acid and jane.

JASON In Greek mythology it was Jason who found the Golden Fleece and wrapped his pet turkey, Harold, in it. Jason is also Nosaj spelled backward, the acronym for National Organization of Southern Actuaries and Jewelers, a paramilitary group out of Birmingham. Nosaj will be meeting October 18 at the Statler Hilton in Roanoke. Rain date October 26.

JAY "Cock of the Walk"—a twentieth-century agreed-upon meaning that was created and paid for by the International Association of Jays in 1922.

JEFF One of the characters from the Commedia dell'Arte. Jeff and his friends Punchinello, Zoonie, and Droxelskewer are known as "The Four Yogurts." Though they do not look like yogurts as we understand them, there has been speculation that because Jeff's feet are made of strawberry jam, and Zoonie's blueberry, and Droxelskewer's boysenberry, and Punchinello's banana, maybe they are yogurts after all. Also, the dates on their foreheads, Jan 10, Mar 4, April 23, and Dec 17, are awfully suspicious.

JENNIFER In Norse mythology Jennifer was the patroness of summer fruit. It was her task to protect the plums and pears and peaches from being eaten. When she failed in this, she was forced by Helvig to hop backward for a year.

JEREMY After the great English philosopher who was reputed to be so smart that hats melted on his head. Jeremys are usually individuals given to pursuits of the intellect—teachers, computer whizzes. Rarely is a good milliner named Jeremy, and when he is he is known as Mr. Jeremy.

JERKROOT The reason everyone wants to be called Jerkroot is not its natural aphrodisiacal properties, but because a dark cloud of toxic gas has been passing overhead. When the cloud disappears, try the name out on your friend and see if it still acts as a sex potion: "Hey, Jerkroot!" Chances are that it won't.

JOAN Joan is usually a nurse. Some Joans, however, are lamps. Especially you, Joan!

JOANNE In folklore Joanne was the little princess who read *National Velvet* and yearned to be a horse. Despite the Queen's protestations she finally got her wish, and at the age of 45 had to be purchased back by the King in a claiming race. Despite having moved down in class all her life, Joanne never finished better than fifth. Letter J—Joanne.

JOE Joe was the little boy who thought he was a firefly and chased hook-and-ladders until he was 26. It was then that his mother explained to him that he was a cretin.

JOEL Greek, "cute chestnut." Joel was the husband of Peeve, the irritating shrew who worked as a rejection manager at a major literary magazine. When Peeve was consumed by her own bile, Joel took to calling himself Marron.

JONATHAN Short for Jonathaniel, which is really Jo-Nathaniel. "Jo" is pronounced "Yo," thus giving us "Yo Nathaniel," or "Hey, Nathaniel, what's up?" Nathaniel is a fancy form of Nathan. See Nathan.

JOY $$$$$$$$$$$$$$, American.

JUAN In history, Don Juan was the irresistible Spanish lover who maintained 100,000 serious relationships at any given time. His career ended suddenly one night when in the dark his trusty prosthetic device got caught in a bear trap, set by a jealous husband, and he was exposed to everyone as a fraud. His source of power gone, Don Juan retired from amorous pursuits and went back to his old job as a drill bit for the Hughes Tool Company.

JULIA After the California cooking prodigy who sailed through Harvard on a home economics fellowship only to perish tragically when her roommate shoved her into a pizza oven. Compounding the tragedy was the fact that her roommate in haste had forgotten both the pepperoni and the mushrooms.

JULIAN Julian was the little tree frog who turned into a handsome prince and promptly bit off the head of Edwina. The King's guards caught Julian hiding in his own pocket and held him fast until his teeth could be filed down to the size of psythes.

JUDY Judy, which means "likely to marry a well-to-do doctor" in ancient Aramaic, was a popular name during the forties and fifties. Famous Judys include Judy Garland, Judy Canova, and Judy Barberuti, who married the top plastic surgeon in her area.

JUNE June, as you know, was named after the month, or the bug. What you may not have known was that the person who originally gave the months their names was a Latino called Jorge. Jorge, pronounced "Horhay," meant "Hune" for June. So if you are interested in accuracy, the month that follows May and comes before Huly is really Hune. In South America, Hune was also the brave hero who saved Rosalita from overdosing on nachos.

JUSTIN Justin is the name of the person who will start World War III. He will do it by accusing the Russians of watering their borscht. Failing this, he is to use a match.

Kk

KAREN Gaelic, "incandescent sex."

KATY From katydid, the cute little insect that descends in clouds on farms and eats everything that isn't nailed down, including the farmers, their wives, their heads, their eyeballs, and everything.

KAY Kay was one of the original eleven letters of the Arabic alphabet, and continues to be so today. Unlike ekpumf, bange, and wee, letters that were dropped from the alphabet after an early blackball, Kay remains comfortably ensconced between J and L, who are almost like brothers to her.

KEITH Keith is the god of the pancreas. Without Keith in one's life most people would stop producing insulin and become diabetic. Modern doctors do not agree that rejection of Keith causes diabetes, but the smart ones cannot rule out the possibility.

KELLY "Leprechaun bites" in Irish. Thus KELLY is found on lawns in Ireland much the way BEWARE OF DOG is found in our own country. This may explain in part why there seem to be so many Kellys in Ireland. If you were to look on the mailbox instead of the lawn, you would find that the people living there were Sullivan.

KENNETH Kenneth was the gay lover of Edwin Drood. There is not much else to say; check your history.

KIM Kim was the Hindu goddess of good taste who fell in love with Ralph Lauren during the fifties and showed him how to mix colors. After Ralph's blistering success with Polo, Kim returned to India to help Ovaltine market red forehead dots to Brahmin women.

LAIRD Laird was the little Norwegian boy who had his schnitzel cut off when he couldn't stop masturbating in front of rabbits. In time, great Odin took pity on Laird and changed everything in the world to rabbits.

LAMPWICK A rare Estonian name meaning "badger droppings" which has somehow found its way to the West. A cadger, a ramicon, a bolt.

LAOCOÖN Still not one of the more popular names, though it is gaining on Bozo.

LAURA Is a name in a misty night, or a misty fog, or a misty pier, or a misty shore, or a misty evening . . .

LAUREN Lauren was the beautiful Rhine maiden who, on a dare, blew a long-stemmed crystal goblet out of a cheese. According to legend she married Gutfreund, the popular gastroenterologist who saved her from Blofarc, the god of bad breath.

LEAKY Modern English, "one who leaks or drips." Leaky is not an attractive name by any standard; in fact, it is downright disgusting. Yuck! Get it away from me.

LEE After Lee Morris Harp, the seventeenth-century British mystic who genuinely believed he was a soap bubble and had to have his fingernails pulled out, one by one, until he was cured. Lee is also the seventh-most-popular name in China, right after Wong and Rin Tin Tin.

LESLEY Lesley is one of those androgynous names that could be either a girl or boy, and sometimes is. "Lesley, I love you. What is that thing, Lesley? Oh, my God, Lesley!" In the eleventh century in France, Lesley was the pretty parsley goddess, who looked in the mirror and noticed she was backwards.

LENNY The last player to run onto the field in any sport. "Hey! Where's Lenny?"

LEO Leo is the patron saint of stationary-bicycle riders. Ten miles, fifteen, twenty, never a worry, Leo is with you. Hadn't you wondered why there are so few accidents among stationary-bicycle riders? No one ever getting run over or hit. Leo, that's why. Leo is one of the least publicized but most effective saints in the business. Because of Leo, stationary-bicycle-riding insurance is practically nonexistent.

LEON According to the Medhaduta, Leon could not contain himself and finally mated with a mountain near his house. To atone for his sin, Leon was sentenced by the citizens of his town to wear a brown "M" on his nose. Despite the fact that Leon told people it stood for "Marty," everyone with an I.Q. over 27 knew the truth.

LILY An abbreviated form of "Lilliput," which was a sixteenth-century lead shot weighing only ½ ounce that Gulliver threw against the little people to build his ego. It is a fact, nevertheless, that in the 1740 Wee Olympics, held in Burdine's pet shop, Gulliver placed dead last in the Lilliput event. Prokoffief, the Russian dwarf, throwing a custom brass lily, took first place.

LINDA "Pretty" in Spanish. Linda spelled backward is Adnil, a leading nasal-decongestant tablet. Lindas for the most part tend to be talkative, fun-loving, and good at stealing husbands. Akin to Lucinda, Linden, Linder, and Lindenroot.

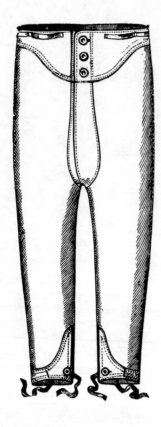

LIONEL "Large growth" in Swedish. "Hey, pal, you've got a lionel behind your ear." Lionel was also the god of wind, who could blow himself up to four times his own size. "My God, Harry, will you look at the size of that Lionel!" Lionels traditionally come in small, medium, and large. Lyon, Lyonell, Lyonil.

LISA In German mythology Lisa was the goddess of chapped lips. It was she who fell in love with Siegfried and made his lips blow up to twice their size after he kissed another woman. No matter how many dragons he slew, Siegfried was never able to reduce the size or tenderness of his lips. Thus the name Lisa has come to mean "she who has power over lips" and is given to girls seeking oral dominion in affairs of the mouth.

LLOYD Lloyd was the co-inventor, in 1737, of the pajama bottom. Before that, no one knew what to wear to church in the morning.

LOLA Lola was the queen of Tyre who dipped her son in wax and used him for a centerpiece at dinner parties. Lola lived a rich and celebrated life, throwing parties and traveling around the world until she was 88, when her son somehow chewed his way out.

LONNY   Lonny is one of those names that you don't find in the paper-and-party stores among the racks of cute little things with names on them that are listed alphabetically. And with good reason: Lonny means "belch" in Old Welsh. The Old Welshmen used to finish a large meal, then get up and eructate loudly, saying "Ah! That was a good Lonny." They didn't know the word eructate.

LORAYNE   "Thunder thighs" in seventeenth-century Castilian Spanish. Lorayne was the princess whose dueña tried to secure her charms against Don Redondo de la Pinca and was crushed to death in the process. Lorayne never did marry Don Redondo and spent the last years of her life lobbying for the Gramm-Rudman bill.

LOUIE   A criminal name made popular in old Chicago, Louie means "slow of mind and strong of grip." True Louies are invariably left-handed and wear dark chalk-striped suits. Their mothers, however, call them Lewis.

LUCIEN   Means either "gumdrop" or "horseshoe" in Black Forest Ogre-ish and during the twelfth century was given to babies or foals. In Baden-Württembers today, about one out of every two persons still carries a Lucien for good luck, while the other gets Lucien stuck in his teeth.

LUCY Ninety-nine point nine percent of all people think of Lucille Ball when the name Lucy is mentioned, which is a shame when you realize that it was not Lucille Ball but David Niven who played Lucy opposite Desi Arnaz on the old *I Love Lucy* show. Of course, not many people know this, which accounts for the persistence of the Lucille Ball association and the blank look when you mention David Niven. But now you know it too, so the next time someone mentions the name Lucy, feel free to visualize David Niven.

LUDWIG German, "big dope." This strong Teutonic name, corrupted from Ludwag, which means "big Dummkopf," is much favored among world-class bull terriers. Just last year Ludwig von Hoenbratten III took Best in Show at Westminster.

LUKE According to legend, Luke was the resourceful boy who kept all the other Eskimos warm during the great blizzard by rubbing their intestines together. Thus, anything that is maintained with a slight temperature elevation has come to be known today as "Luke Warm." Luke is also the twelfth letter in the French alphabet.

LULU Lulu means "can-can" in French. Thus all can-can dancers are named Lulu. Why they aren't called Lu-Lu dancers is anybody's guess.

LYNN   Lynn was and still is the Roman goddess of bathrobes. Next time you buy a bathrobe you will notice a little slip of paper as you unwrap it that reads, "Inspected by #34." That's Lynn.

Mm

MAC A name created by the ancients to go with "Hey" or "Big."

MAGNUS This mighty name is from the Latin magnum, "double bottle," and in it are implied respect, awe, and grandeur. To have a baby named Magnus is equivalent to having two babies of any other name. Some families aspire to Jeroboam, Rehoboam, and Methuselah.

MANDY Mandy means "chocolate candy" in every language, but especially in the third grade.

MARCELLA "Reef dweller," Italian. In Italian folklore, Marcella was the Neapolitan virgin who truly believed God could snorkle and, acting on this belief, created and developed the exciting underwater-sporting-equipment world of Sears, Roebuck. At the age of 73, Marcella's mind snapped and she began to hide behind the counter and bite customers who came into her department not wearing flippers. Sensitive to her plight, Sears executives voted to buy her a little place on the coral reef where she could live out her years rather than have her mounted.

MARCIA "Lively bullfinch" in Early Territorial Dutch. Marcia was the strange sorceress who on a dare could swallow herself.

MARCUS Marcus is the stuff that comes out of a squirrel when it gets run over in the street. In the ancient world, it was the fifth humour after blood, phlegm, bile, and lymph.

MARIA Maria was the nympho sister of Oliver Twist. When confronted with any problem larger than lunch, Maria would head for the bedroom. To her credit, Maria smoked. Marie, Marianne, Marionette.

MARK Contemporary American. A dot or small sign, generally in pencil or dirt.

MARLENE Marlene is a soft cream that Frenchwomen apply to their cheeks to get rid of the tattoos that say U.S. NAVY and MOTHER. In history, Marlene was the daughter of Phhht, the reclusive World War II cryptologist who encoded himself and was never found.

MARSHA Shortened from the Old Italian "Marshamellow," meaning short, sweet, fluffy, and white, Marsha has come to mean short. Old Italian lingual relatives are marshagrass (short grass), marshagas (short gas), marshahare (short hare). Marsha was also the goddess of paper in the Pan-Druid culture.

MARTIN Martin was the folk hero who proved invulnerable to IRS audits during the tax pogroms of the 1940s. Despite an orgy of unprovoked persecution over his '45 and '46 returns, Martin survived unscathed. He attributed his good fortune to eating large quantities of carrots and other yellow vegetables.

MARY Biblical, "pie."

MARY ANN "Strawberry pie."

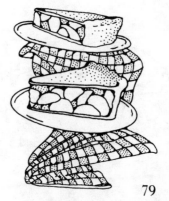

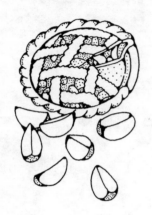

MARY BETH "Blueberry pie."

MARY ELIZABETH "Cherry pie."

MARY JANE "Rhubarb pie."

MARY JO "Peach pie."

MARY KAY "Apple pie."

MARY LOU "Banana cream pie."

MATTHEW The only nonspider to be awarded the Order of Merit for the quality of his webs, Matthew was bitten by a poisonous rival in 1978 and died a hideous death. Thus Matthew has come to mean "Aieeeeee! No, no! Arrghhh!" in English.

MAURA "Ventral fin," as in the old nautical line "Don't show your Maura to me, pal!" Maura can also mean "beautiful jazz singer."

MAUREEN Irish country dialect for "strawberry shortcake." Because of their red hair, Maureens are often mistaken for desserts and forced to march against their wills as drum majorettes in the Saint Patrick's Day parade. On the sidelines, lusty men—construction workers, lumberjacks, and football players—wait with pails of whipped cream.

MAXINE Maxine Liverpullet of Peoria, Illinois, was at one time the fastest stitch in the world. During the Depression, on orders from President Roosevelt himself, Maxine knitted socks for the entire U.S. Army within ten days. Years later, suffering from a severe case of yarn fever, Maxine knitted herself into a cocoon and was never heard from again.

MEADE Meade was the illegitimate cousin of Ed Koch who was taught early in life to read only ball bearings. At the age of 46, Meade bolted from this narrow view of belles lettres and read two bowling balls and some shot on a dare.

MEGAN The sister of Filch, who lost control of herself and blew hot wax into the ear of the Emperor. When the Emperor beheaded Filch, Megan licked his toes and begged forgiveness. Impressed by her sincerity and good looks, the Emperor asked Megan to lick the wax out of his ears. Thus among French goatherds, Megan has become synonymous with "ear floss."

MELISSA Melissa, or "steamed lotus blossom" in Island French, goes well with the last name Oolalani Lani, which means "Feldman" in Hawaiian. This fact was apparently picked up in Scarsdale, where at last count three-quarters of the first grade at Scarsdale Elementary School were named Melissa Oolalani Lani. Literary buffs may also remember that Melissa was the bride of Welkin in the Clifford Odets play *Danny Potato*.

MELVIN Melvin was the lucky gamester who got the greens and Boardwalk every time he played Monopoly and killed everybody else. Nor would he let you off if you landed on one of his railroads or utilities. Melvin had difficulty making friends, however, because of a personality defect, and tried to commit suicide by selling his co-op for less than $2 million.

MIKE Old Electronic for "voice amplifier." Mikes generally have loud voices and metal teeth. People who like to putter around with electricity and former radio announcers tend to name their offspring Mike. The name was popularized during the thirties by the famous twins Mike Peterson and Mike Moscowitz. Also Michael, Mick, Muk, Harold.

MILDRED Mildred was the goddess of cheap bedding and laundry. Most hotel chains know Mildred, as do hospitals and people who shop the basement at Alexander's. Mildred tried once to move up to designer spreads, but Zeus, in a fit of anger, hurled her from Olympus right into the Housekeeping department of the Hilton chain. Mildred was so angry at Zeus she stayed there to teach him a lesson, and hoped he would check in so she could French his bed. No luck. Zeus never showed up, and Mildred stayed at Hilton forever, finally marrying Sergio, the god of security.

MILLY Depends to some extent on whether it derives from Millicent or from Mildred. By itself, Milly just means "half mild, half silly," in the same way that "Tom" is half Tim, half Dom, and the Hubble constant involves the Red Shift. To the best of my knowledge, though, all Millys share a love of plum pudding. Also Millie, Millipede, Militant.

MINDY Portuguese, short for "Mindywine." In Portugal everyone drinks a glass of Mindy before going to sleep. It is the Mindy that helps the Portuguese dream that they are really Spanish.

MIRANDA A sorceress, yes; tempestuous and bewitching, of course; but also one hell of a wrestling coach. Miranda's all-dwarf wrestling team from the Devil section of East Flatbush finished first in this year's Olympic trials. Miranda herself, in a fit of rage, tied one of the opposing coaches into an eternal clove hitch.

MOE Few people are named Moe anymore, thanks primarily to the good work of the American Psychiatric Association. In a longitudinal study conducted between 1896 and 1986 it was found that more Moes smoke large cigars—El Presidentes and hand-rolled Havanas—than any other name. Sols and Vitos did okay too.

MORRIS Made famous by Morris Wildskin, the man who invented the live cummerbund, Morris is a name worn with pride and distinction. In case you were wondering, Morris the cat is spelled with three *r*'s.

MORTY As you probably know, a "morty" is a rose-colored mole that grows in the shape of a toilet seat along your neck, where it eventually strangles you. Too bad if you have one.

MOSES Biblical. Moses was one of the great leaders of Israel. With the guidance of his patron, God, Moses negotiated the controversial release of the Hebrews from Egypt and led them into the wilderness. On Mount Sinai he and God wrote the celebrated document *Ten Commandments,* which helped unite the people of Israel and for which they earned the Nobel Peace Prize.

MOWGLI Mowgli was the name Kipling gave to the man-child in *The Jungle Book,* though researchers have learned that his true name was Marvin. For what it's worth, Marvin was never really scared of Shere Khan, though Kaa gave him the willies.

MUFFIN Muffin, which is essentially a cutesy little teddy-bear name, falls into the same class as Doodoo and Cuff Cuff. Muffins are flirters and eye batters. Most people on meeting a Muffin for the first time have to fight off the impulse to kick her down a flight of stairs.

MURRAY Murray was the sturgeon king in ancient Sumer. Very few babies today are named Murray, since it's hard to become a sturgeon king, and wear a white apron, and say "Number 95?" when you're a baby.

MYRA Myra was the Phoenician goddess of ethnic jokes. It was Myra who told the first Polish story, the one about how many Poles it would take to screw in a light bulb. Definitely a goddess for all seasons, she could do stand-up with the best of them and wither any heckler with a killer remark. Myra is remembered best for her classic lines "Funny, you don't look Jewish" and "Ah, so!" She was married to Frith, the god of power steering.

Nn

NANCY Nancy means "nice-smelling" in Pidgin English. If you've never smelled a fresh Nancy before, you're in for a real treat. Sort of a cross between hot corn bread and musk. On a personal note, I have never come across a bad-smelling Nancy; Nancys just always smell good.

NAOMI In the Bible, Naomi was the only one who knew for sure that the Great Pyramid of Khufuw was built by Donald Trump. Unable to contain this information, she burst all over Canaan.

NATALIE From the Czech verb natal, "to kiss." Natalie (kiss me), Natalou (kiss you), Nataler (kiss her), Natalus (kiss us), Natalem (kiss them).

NATASHA Natasha was the seductive KGB agent who wore Aunt Jemima pancake syrup behind her ears instead of cologne. She was apprehended by the CIA in 1981 and forced to become a free-lance writer.

NATHAN Nathan means "he who naths" in Hebrew. According to the Bible, Nathan nathed Samuel and was sent into the desert for seven years and forty nights. Not until he figured out just how one spends seven years and forty nights someplace did God allow Nathan to return to his tree house in Jerusalem.

NEIL As a youngster you will be taunted with "Neil, Neil, potato peel." Do not let this get you down or depress you. You are not a potato peel.

NICK From the Latin "No que crosse Nickere, si no face formaggio," which means "Don't cross Nick if you don't want to end up like a cheese."

NOAH Biblical. Noah was the hero who saved both man and beast from the Great Flood. A boatwright by profession, Noah spent nine months aboard his great ark, *Hilda II,* with seven pairs of every clean creature after the catastrophic forty-day-and-forty-night deluge. He was credited with having extracted a promise from you know Who never again to destroy the world in a fit of rage.

NOEL Noel, the converse of Leon, was the court jester to Hipster IV of Nantucket. His favorite trick, which never failed to send Hipster into paroxysms of laughter, was to stick a rifle up his nose and threaten to pull the trigger.

NORA Nora Cassaloric was the marketing genius who founded Teeth 'R' Us, the giant dental clinic in Paramus which in 1983 alone filled more than 600,000 cavities. To this day, anyone with the name Nora who is a resident of New Jersey can go to Teeth 'R' Us between 2 and 4 A.M. Monday through Saturday, and receive free dental treatment.

NORMAN After Norman Mailer, the great twentieth-century novelist and president of PEN, who beat the daylights out of Harold of England at the Battle of Hastings in 1066 to consolidate his empire, and recorded it all in *The Executioner's Song*.

NORTON If your name is Norton, it might as well be Noogan, or Niblet, because people are all going to tease you anyway. "Hey, Norty-Snorty," they will say, secure in the knowledge that they are Charlie, or Steve, or Rock. Thank God you are the 6-foot-6-inch Black Belt crazed steel strong arm for Attila the Hun who chews up Pittsburgh Steelers linemen two at a time just for fun and spent ten years in Attica for manslaughter. Kick their ass.

OGDEN Ogden was the 800-pound mushroom in *The Garden of the Finzi-Continis* that was the source of their power.

OLIVIA The Greek goddess of mayonnaise who, in a weak moment, told her recipe to Hellmann, her lover.

OONA Oona was the Aleut maiden who fell in love with a polar bear and used every trick in the book to attract his attention, including wearing no underpants. Unfortunately for Oona, it worked. Oona, ona, na, a . . .

OONOO Oonoo will be the name of the first intelligent being from another world to make contact with us through a binary palimpsest over a radio telescope. The message will read: "Sorry, but I'm dead now. Please communicate with my great-grandson, at 1 (403) 555-6191 in the Crab Nebula, and inform him that you have received this message. By the time your transmission reaches him you will probably be dead as well, so send us the probable name of your great-grandchild so that we can keep this conversation going. Regards, Oonoo."

OTIS Otis was the Roman god of canned fruit who in return for 12 cases of figs in heavy syrup extracted a promise from Apollo that his name would appear in commuter elevators until the year 2000.

Pp

PABLO Spanish for Gdansk. Pablos often prefer to be called olbaP, which is Pablo backward, or ksnadG, which is Gdansk backward. Dyslexics will have no difficulty with this. Among true intimates the great Picasso was known as ksnadG, or sometimes affectionately as olbaP, and if you read his signature backward, as he often urged people to do, you will see "ossaciP olbaP."

PAM Pam was the mythological satyr who played the pipes in the forest at night.

PATRICIA Patricia was the magnificent therapist who in a fit of empathy absorbed all the neuroses in the world. Until she burst from overload in 1937, no one ever worried, or screamed at anyone else, or was kinky. Believe it.

PATRICK Patrick was the only saint who could still paint a green line down the center of the street after chug-a-lugging 5 quarts of beer. Thrilled beyond belief about Patrick's artistic talent, God turned Patrick into a pot of gold and used him to buy more beer. Pat, Pat my boy, Patsy.

PAUL Paul was the Czechoslovakian god of the hearth from 1863 to 1874. During his short reign Paul sired many Czech children, from whom all modern children named Paul are descended. If your name is Paul, Pauli, or Paula, chances are your great-grandmother got to know the Czech god Paul personally.

PAYNE While the name Payne suggests rich traditions and good breeding, you and I know that most Paynes trace their beginnings to one Jack Pain who even then was known to townspeople as Swift. So come off it, Payne, will you?

PEARL From "poil," an opalescent bead found in an oyster at Gargulio's restaurant in Coney Island in 1922.

PEGGY Short for "Pegoinette." Pegoinette was the creator of Elefoncil, the enormous tranquilizer dart that was used to sedate South America.

PENUS Stop that! Don't even think it for a moment. That's spelled with an *i* not a *u*, you dope. Penus was the Venetian god of catheters, whose picture was hung in all major hospitals above the THIS WAY TO CAFETERIA sign. I can't believe you thought what you thought. Don't they educate people anymore? Ye gods!

PETER Many famous people bear the name Peter, among them Peter the Great, Peter Pan, Saint Peter, and Peter O'Toole. The one thing they all have in common is the uncanny ability to kiss themselves on the back of the neck.

PHILIP After Philip of Macedon, who was the first person ever to be removed from a bus because he had no head.

PHOEBE Phoebe, pronounced "Marilyn," was the Swedish garden troll who prevented Buicks from molesting the flowers at night.

PIERPONT "Blank check" in Neo-Latin. Pierponts tend to have unlimited resources upon which they can draw. Family's investment bank, trust funds, that sort of thing. What is not generally known about Pierponts is that they are a little kinky. Electricity, cross-dressing . . . shhh!

PIERRE Pierre is an artificial name manufactured exclusively by the Namograph company for use by maître d's in restaurants and hotels. Also Duardo, Gino.

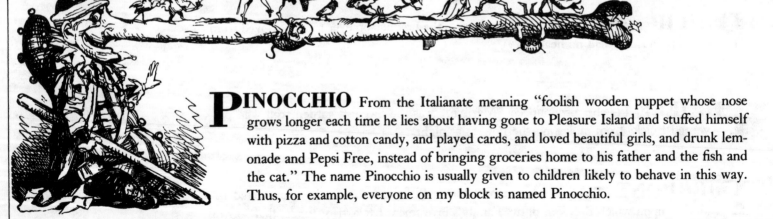

PINOCCHIO From the Italianate meaning "foolish wooden puppet whose nose grows longer each time he lies about having gone to Pleasure Island and stuffed himself with pizza and cotton candy, and played cards, and loved beautiful girls, and drunk lemonade and Pepsi Free, instead of bringing groceries home to his father and the fish and the cat." The name Pinocchio is usually given to children likely to behave in this way. Thus, for example, everyone on my block is named Pinocchio.

PLUCKY I liked the name Plucky so much I took it out of the book and ate it. If the particular edition you are reading has Plucky in it, it is a misprint.

POKEY Pokey's cute, Pokey's slow, or so it is claimed. In point of fact, Pokey's no slower than anyone else, certainly not Harley Bogwald, and the name is short for "pokendokesis," an annoying virus that was virulent and rampant in the South during the Civil War. Sufferers from pokendokesis apparently broke out in seeds all over their bodies and looked like large strawberries. Unlike strawberries, however, they tasted sour.

POLLY Let's dispel the myth once and for all. Polly is not a parrot. Polly is an elephant. Want a peanut, Polly?

Qq

QUILKIN Suffice that it was the knight Quilkin who forgot to wear an athletic supporter during his turn at the lists. Quilkin did survive, however, and changed his name to Darlene.

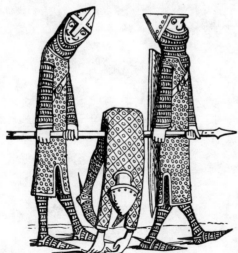

99

Rr

RAIN-IN-THE-FACE From the Hebrew "spritz in punim." Rain-in-the-Face continues to be one of the more popular Jewish names, even today.

RALPH "Strictly Bloomingdale's," as David Pearce would say. Yes, that David Pearce.

RAMBO Rambo isn't necessarily a first name, but people use it as a first name. The original Rambo is a killer misanthrope, a cross between a wolverine and a Green Beret snapping turtle, created by Colonel Trautman and kept in a steel cage 700 feet below Boulder Dam. The Army keeps him there for safety during peacetime. Trautman is the only person Rambo trusts. If Trautman says "Fetch," Rambo fetches. If Trautman says "Kill," Rambo kills. For the most part Trautman uses Rambo to bring the newspaper in from the front porch, though occasionally he lets him attack a Mafia family or Third

World nation just for practice. If your child is a Milquetoast with glasses, I would avoid naming him Rambo. Maybe you could name him Trautman.

RAQUEL Raquel was the Brazilian princess who could carve *The Sun Also Rises* onto a Grape Nut and still leave room for a limerick or two. She was also the mistress of Fernando the Fruitcake, who loved to have her sew labels into his underwear that only ants could read.

RAYMOND Raymond, or Ray, as he likes to be called, means "Adios Hanover to win in the third," and is the most frequently encountered name at Volvo service centers. If you doubt this even for a moment, take your car in for a tune-up and ask for Ray. Tell him I sent you, and that you need the car back by Thursday.

REBECCA Ancient Hebrew for "Elizabeth Taylor." Rebecca was the beautiful dark-eyed Jewess that everybody knows Ivanhoe really wanted but couldn't have so he settled for faithful, proper Rowena, and married her and had lots of little children named Sir this and Lady that. George Sanders, for his part, finally got so fed up with Rebecca and her standing on the parapet wall and threatening to jump that he married Zsa Zsa Gabor and lived happily ever after for a week.

REDUX Next to Lisa and Michael, Redux is the most popular name of the eighties. Latin for "dux again," Redux is the name of choice among college-educated Spanish can-can dancers.

REGIS After Saint Regis, the Roman soldier who won a Westinghouse science talent scholarship for his project "Use of the Cattle Prod with Recalcitrant Adolescents," and was canonized by grateful parents.

RENÉ Old French, "wise trellis." However, in Latin René means "he barks." René House (He barks at the house), René Mailman (He barks at the mailman), René Lamb Chop (He barks at the lamb chop).

RHODA "Fat pot roast" in German. Rhoda was the Rhine maiden who in any fair contest could drink the University of Pennsylvania football team under the table. During World War II Rhoda was called into service as an oil tanker.

RICHARD Richard was not only the lion-hearted Saxon king, brother of the evil Prince John, he was the first person ever to make contact with an alien intelligence from outer space named Bruce. Wisely, Richard never mentioned this to anyone except Carl Sagan.

RICKY The feeble attempt of stupid babies to say "Richard."
"Snookums, this is Richard. Say hello to Richard, Snookums."
"Ricky, Ricky."
"Good, Snookums. Now stop biting Richard's leg."

RITA Rita was the Roman goddess of bronchial tubes. During the January-February flu season, Rita would come out into the open and personally direct the fever and coughing spasms of prominent Roman senators and their wives. As if in gratitude for this attention, the aristocrats would frequently heave their guts out.

ROBERTA Roberta was the Queen of rubber gloves, who on a moment's notice could produce a pair that would fit any size from 6 to 13. "Finger Fashion" is what Roberta called her gloves, and she sold them to better department stores everywhere. If you have a pair of rubber gloves in the kitchen drawer, chances are they are a pair of Roberta's, and even if they're not, Roberta can probably tell you how many fingers they have, nine times out of ten.

GLOVE FITTING

ROBIN Nouvelle Dutch. After the bird that arrives in spring and immediately begins to sing—tweet, tweet, tweet tweet, tweet, tweet tweet, as if to say, "Look at me, I don't have monthly mortgage payments to meet, or April taxes, or stomach acid, tweet tweet." "Tweet tweet" is roughly equivalent to "Ha! ha!" and is usually sung in a mocking tone.

ROCK After an enormous Egyptian boulder in Southern Colorado. People named Rock generally exude the personality characteristics and sensibilities of their namesake.
"You sad, Rock?"
"Naw, not me."
"You happy, Rock?"
"Get lost!"
Rocks do not, for example, dance ballet, play the flute, or do calligraphy. Rocks do work with medicine balls, hold up stanchions, and box. Famous Rocks: Rock Hudson, Rock of Gibraltar, Rocky, Rockaway, Rockette, Rockule.

ROCKBOURNE The ultimate name. Studies have shown that Rockbourne is everything you could possibly want in a name. Say it and get the feel of it, "Rockbourne, Rockbourne, Rockbourne." Don't you just love it?

ROGER Roger comes from the French roger and means "10-4," or "okay," in communicationese. Why a pilot answers an instruction from the control tower with "Roger" and not "Harvey" is anyone's guess. Perhaps Roger knows someone at the control tower, or maybe even higher up. Roger may be very well connected; in fact—Why should I kid you?—I know he is.

RONNIE Ronnie is the abbreviated form of Ronnieskinweltzesmirchbezen, which means "blintz" in German. Throughout Bavaria, one can hear waiters shouting to short-order cooks, "Pair of ronnies with jelly and sour cream and a tuna down." Who the hell knows what they're talking about?

ROSE Despite the fact that you may have thought your Aunt Rose was named after the flower, it is the other way around. The flower was named after Aunt Rose, who has been around longer than she'd care to recount, and was indeed a source of inspiration to Shakespeare and other poets. It is interesting to note that Rose is the surname of Pete Rose, the baseball player, who was also named after your Aunt Rose. Little did you suspect, eh?

ROVER Rover is a canine name applied to persons who like to bring the paper into the house with their teeth. If they sit up and beg as well, you might want to consider calling them Fido or Spot.

ROY Roy is not a standard name like Groucho or Wenceslas; rather, it is an unusual Caucasoid name meaning "Lean to the left, lean to the right, stand up, sit down, fight, fight, fight!" Thus it is hardly surprising to see someone at a football game shout "Roy! Roy!" at the top of his lungs, and then pour salt down the neck of the person in front of him.

RUCKUS Ruckus was the Roman god of noise, who in his exuberance gave mankind too many groups. Fortunately, great Wonka sent down headphones, the angel of quiet, to rectify the matter. Had Ruckus had his way, every teenager in America today would be locking himself in his room after dinner and playing jungle rhythms at 2,000 decibels.

RUDOLPH Popular among reindeer; a little risky for humans.

RUTH

RUTH Ruth was the first person ever to have memorized an entire language, French. What is even more remarkable is that she memorized it in Spanish.

Ss

SALLY "Sad egg cup" in Middle Moravian Dutch, Sally is also a variation of Silly, after the mad empress of Yugoslavia who used to talk to her bicycle seat.

SANDY Sandy was originally Solveig, the goddess of sensual pleasures, until great Olaf, unable to contain himself, anointed her with butter and rolled her along the beach.

SCOTT "Irresistible to girls." Never in the history of the world has a Scott failed to melt the defenses of even the most intransigent of virgins, just by mentioning his name. "Hi, I'm Scott." Swoon. Why this is, no one knows.

SHARON All Sharons are descended from Ariel Sharon, who is much older than he looks. If you should meet the jolly former Defense Minister of Israel while traveling through the Middle East, feel free to introduce yourself to him as one of his long-lost great-great-granddaughters. No doubt he will laugh good-naturedly at this remark and order an air strike against Palestinian fighter units living in your navel.

SATYR Out of alphabetical order, and more a description than a name. The satyr is a mythological beast composed of a demi-savage united to the hind legs of a goat which has the stamina of a modern-day steam engine. Curiously, if you turn a satyr upside down you get a woodpecker. Despite their reputation for being sexually aggressive, satyrs are actually peaceful creatures who will not attack another animal unless it exists. Duck! Here comes one now.

SHEILA Sheila the Cute Stuff, in Hinduism, was the fourth member of the quatri-murti along with Shiva the Destroyer, Brahma the Creator, and Vishnu the Preserver. The problem with Sheila the Cute Stuff was that she had 12 arms and would never let you go, even if you had to go to the bathroom, so that many people perished in her arms. Thus the Bhagavad Gita asks the question "Is it worth getting involved with Cute Stuff if you know in advance you're going to die with Cute Stuff?" Many people think not.

SHIRLEY Shirley was the second-favorite odalisque of Sheik Mamoud al-Fahd, who liked the way she talked dirty. After leaving Sheik Mamoud's harem in 1934 to do a stint as a truck driver, Shirley had her name legally changed to Belle Barth.

SHMEIRDLICH Shmeirdlich, which is the Hindu equivalent of "Shnerdpuss," has never caught on here in the West despite its obvious romantic qualities. Shmeirdlich was the daughter of Kvetch who ran off with a moonbeam and was kept under heavy sedation till the end of time.

STANISLAW Stanislaw is hardly related to cole slaw at all. Whereas cole slaw is chopped-up cabbage and carrots in a mayonnaise base, Stanislaw is a lieutenant in the Polish Army—a minor distinction, to be sure, but a distinction nonetheless. Stanislaw does like cole slaw, however, and uses it to insulate his house. What makes Stanislaw interesting is that he was the first Polish soldier to get a tank pregnant. Stanczak, Stankiewicz, Stanko, Stupido.

STANLEY Stanleys, as you probably all know, come from the Isle of Stan in the South Pacific Ocean where everyone is named Stanley, even the women. To the best of my knowledge there are no other Stanleys anywhere in the world.

STEPHANIE Stephanie was the rich little Danish princess who spent $2.5 million of her February allowance to have herself made over into a Ping-Pong ball. Unfortunately, today no one knows which one she is. King Gustav and Queen Castrella of Denmark have urged all players to slam every shot they can until Stephanie is found.

STEVE From the Greek stevatos, "to cook." Steve means literally "to cook oneself." Steve, Stevie, Steve Pal all mean "to cook oneself." Stevedore, on the other hand, means "to adore him who cooks himself." Stephen, Steven, Steeven.

STUART After Stuart Warfel, the first person ever to have received a life sentence for foxing books.

SUSAN Susan was the Greek goddess of laughter, who would break up if someone so much as stepped on a jellyfish at the beach and got stung. Today's Susans, however, have lost much of the playful sense of humor of their namesake, and don't even find divorce funny, or cardiac arrhythmia.

SY Sy, or Seymour, was the legendary gin rummy player who was so good he could get under two before the cards were dealt. No one would play with him, not even retired furriers and sportswear manufacturers living in Florida. Thus, "The Scourge of the Beach" as he was known, had to hustle games under false names, like Moe, and Irving, and Sol. Sy was killed by shrapnel in 1959 when a furniture salesman he had lured into a game ginned in his face.

Tt

TARA Literally "Fear of seersucker" in Latin. Many people suffer from Tara, though it is more common in tropical climates.

TERRY "Regal buttock" in Tri-German, Terry was the name given to slightly irregular Prussian children as punishment. Terry was also the winged phantom in *The Marriage of Figaro* who could crash into walls headfirst at 700 miles per hour and only destroy his head.

THAYER Thayer means "whistle row" in Levantine German. Unfortunately, no one seems to know what "whistle row" means, or for that matter who the Levantine Germans were, or for that matter why someone would be named Thayer in the absence of such knowledge. Nevertheless, it is a pretty name, especially when paired with Drilkinstep as a surname.

TIM A corruption of the Old English thim, which means absolutely nothing. Tim has come to mean Mit spelled backward. It is interesting to note, though too much should not be made of it, that at King Arthur's Round Table none of the knights were named Tim. But for that matter, none of the knights were named Larry either.

TINA Tina was the early Indian feminist who chased Yellow Deer up a tree before taking his job away from him. A hard-liner with words as well as fists, she is remembered best for her militant column, "Sioux View," which advocated circumcising enemy braves in addition to scalping them.

TONY "Tortellini-head" in Italian. Tonys are invariably identified with the wrong pasta by four- and five-year-old peers who go "Tony is a macaroni, Tony is a macaroni" ad nauseum.

TRACY Tracy was the beautiful Trojan queen whose gift for typing rapidly with her left foot was the marvel of the ancient world. When Achilles came to pay her homage, Tracy typed the word AWESOME all over his face.

TREVOR After Sir Howard Trevor-Greystoke, the English psychiatrist who treated his famous nephew Tarzan for years until he got him over his small, cute bird fetish.

TRUDY During World War II, Trudy was the bait used to coax tanks into the fray the same way mechanical rabbits are used at racetracks with greyhounds.

Uu

ULALUME French, "umbrella trap." Edgar Allan Poe wrote a beautiful poem about an umbrella trap, which, not unexpectedly, he titled "Ulalume."

ULYSSES Ulysses was the great Greek hero who in real life intentionally steered his ship into the sirens and beat the cyclops to death with a stick. He was a sadistic son of a bitch and should be struck from the Odyssey.

Vv

VANESSA "Houri's houri." Arabic equivalent of "crème de la crème."

VERONICA The name of a dangerous move which means "fool the bull" in Spanish. Bullfighters often execute half and full verónicas to lull the bull into a state of hypnotic inactivity. The great matador El Pinguín, to demonstrate his control over the bull, once performed a full verónica on Berzerko, the Crazed One, then turned his back and walked away. The recovery team found part of El Pinguín in the bush country near Madrid the next day, and the rest of him in Barcelona.

VICKI Vicki was the Swiss goddess of cheese who was melted down into lava and used to serve up to ten people. Among the illiterate community, she is known simply as Fondue.

VICTOR Victor means "porky" in Greek, and is given to people who most closely resemble the state of Utah. According to legend, Victor searched mightily for Protor, his enemy, then tied his shoelaces together when he found him.

VIOLET After the steam engine.

VIRGINIA Virgins have disappeared from the face of the earth, the last one having been deflowered in March of 1985, so there is no longer a need for a state called Virginia. There is a need for a state called Lila, however.

VIVIAN After Viviana Portulaca, the brilliant Italian linguist who first translated the poetry of President Idi Amin into English from the original Gibberish.

W w

WALCOX Walcox is indeed a name, which unfortunately has been classified Top Secret by the Pentagon. In fact, I had to get several security clearances just to mention it here. "Walcox, *Walcox,* WALCOX!"

WALTER Walter means "wigsfoot" in French. Botanical name for the yellow-flowering wig, or "herb of grace," which victors (see Victor) used in ancient times to stuff up the nose of a fallen enemy just before stamping on him.

WARREN Where rabbits used to live before Rabbits' Lib.

WAYNE After the demotic hero of the *Wayniad*, who survived the attack of the killer fund-raisers only to be outspent by Boesky, the giant stockbroker who splurged every chance he got and with whom Wayne had been trying to keep up for thirty years.

WENDY English colloquial for "she who knows how to negotiate crowds," Wendy was actually the James M. Barrie character who lived with Peter Pan for two difficult years before realizing that he was gay. When the painful discovery was made, in a lingerie shop on West 4th Street, Wendy immediately took up with Captain Hook. Variations: Windy, Wendle, Mrs. C. Hook.

WERTHER First encountered by most people in Goethe's Erziehungsroman *Die Leiden des jungen Werthers*, Werther is really a corruption of "weather," as in "What's the weather today, Harry?" As far as we can tell, the weather was never any good, even in Goethe's time. Rain, snow, sleet, blech! Werthe, Werether, Dr. Frank Field.

WHISTPIFFLE An exceedingly rare English name meaning "air bubble" or something like that, which only recently fetched $200,000 at auction.

WILLIAM American Indian, "Rain upside yo head." With his aggressive "no feather" policy, the great Sioux chief William the Conqueror cleaned up the old Southwest of all Blackfoots, Yellowcheeks, and Apaches in 1099.

WILLY NILLY One of the famous Nilly brothers, Willy Nilly, Billy Nilly, Silly Nilly, and Ramon.

WINGSTABLER See Hatchraven.

WOODY Woody was the eighth dwarf, after Doc, Grumpy, Sleepy, Bashful, Dopey, Jumpy, and Mike.

Yy

YVETTE Yvette is French for "screwdriver," as in "Passez-moi l'yvette, s'il vous plaît." Okay, okay, so you looked it up in Cassell's and it's not listed. Would you believe it means "lil Yve" in français ancien? It really does, but unfortunately no one speaks français ancien anymore. Thus your only choice is to trust me. Trust me: it means "screwdriver." If you ask for an "yvette" and they pass you a wrench, they're probably just not fluent in French.

YVONNE Yvonne was the second wife of Henry, King of Celts, who locked himself in a jar to keep from spoiling. Yvonnes are, by and large, "easy giggles," and left to their own devices tend to wiggle and bob if not weighted down.

Zz

ZBIGNIEW Polish. To designate something large and recent, as in "Have you seen zbigniew nose on Sophie?"

ZENA Zena was the Greek goddess of dust, who on any given day could whip up a storm that would strike terror into the hearts of grown men. Imagine walking slowly along a deserted road when suddenly, out of nowhere, a whirling, swirling, Kansas twister comes at you, and picks you up, and carries you high into the air, and through the sky, burning your eyes and getting into your ears, and doesn't set you down again until you are back where you belong, with Toto and Aunt Em. It was most likely Zena.

ZOË Greek. The feminine of Joë. If the Yankee Clipper had been female, he would have been Zoë DiMaggio.

AUTHOR'S NOTE

The etymologies in this book are absolutely true, so help me God!

ABOUT THE AUTHOR

Lewis Frumkes is a throwback to another era when people did names instead of drugs. In this sense he considers himself a renaissance man. He also writes gently looney essays for the likes of *Punch*, *Harper's Magazine*, and *The New York Times*. When not writing essays or books he likes to dress up as a giant kumquat and scare his neighbors, though he says there is less and less time for that sort of thing nowadays. At present Frumkes lives in New York with his wife and two children and, according to at least one observer, bears a remarkable resemblance to Fred Flintstone.